COUNT WITH THE PIRATES!

AHOY ME HEARTIES AND WELCOME TO YOUR PIRATE PUZZLE BOOK!

GET YOUR COUNTING SKILLS AT THE READY AND OFF YOU GO...

How many skull and cross bones can you see?

THERE ARE 4 SKULL AND CROSS BONES!

How many swords are here?

THERE ARE 6 SWORDS HERE!

What animal do you see more of?

THERE ARE MORE SHARKS!

7 Sharks

3 Parrots

3 Fish

2 Octopuses

1 Turtle

How many messages in bottles did Pirate Jack see on his way to the treasure?

PIRATE JACK SAW 4 MESSAGES IN BOTTLES!

There are 3 pirates with red hats

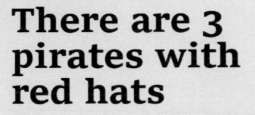

There are 2 pirates with red bandanas

= 5

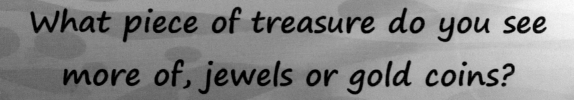

What piece of treasure do you see more of, jewels or gold coins?

THERE ARE MORE GOLD COINS!

10
gold coins

7 jewels

How many coconuts
fell from the trees while
Pirate Pete was sleeping?

9 COCONUTS FELL FROM THE TREES!

THERE ARE 8 MERMAIDS!

What can you
see more of,
pirate boats or
pirate ships?

THERE ARE MORE PIRATE BOATS!

6 pirate boats

4 pirate ships

Captain Goldbeard has made off with some treasure, but how many gold cups did he have to leave behind?

CAPTAIN GOLDBEARD HAD TO LEAVE 4 GOLD CUPS BEHIND!

How many pirates are wanted?

THERE ARE 6 WANTED PIRATES!

WANTED
DEAD OR ALIVE
EXTREMELY DANGEROUS
EXTREME CAUTION SHOULD BE EXERCISED
$3,500 REWARD

WANTED
DEAD or ALIVE
10,000$

WANTED
Pirate Percy
REWARD
$ 1,000,000

REWARD
WANTED
DEAD OR ALIVE
$100,000 REWARD

WANTED
$10,000 REWARD
ARMED AND VERY DANGEROUS
CASH REWARD

WANTED
DEAD OR ALIVE
EXTREMELY DANGEROUS
EXTREME CAUTION SHOULD BE EXERCISED
$3,500 REWARD

How many flags can you see on the map?

THE LOST TREASURE

There are 7 flags

THERE ARE **5** TREASURE CHESTS!

How many chicken legs has Captain Flynn taken a bite out of?

CAPTAIN FLYNN'S TAKEN A BITE OUT OF

10

CHICKEN LEGS!

How many pirates can you see?

THERE ARE
6
PIRATES!

Made in the USA
Middletown, DE
07 February 2020